T0128414

ANALYZING THE FAIR MARKET VALUE OF ASSETS AND THE STAKEHOLDERS' INVESTMENT DECISIONS

DISSERTATION

SUBMITTED TO NORTHCENTRAL UNIVERSITY

GRADUATE FACULTY OF THE SCHOOL OF BUSINESS AND TECHNOLOGY MANAGEMENT IN PARTIAL FULFILLMENT OF THE REQUIREMENTS FOR THE DEGREE OF

DOCTOR OF BUSINESS ADMINISTRATION

DR. ANIS I. MILAD

authorHOUSE®

AuthorHouse™
1663 Liberty Drive
Bloomington, IN 47403
www.authorhouse.com
Phone: 1 (800) 839-8640

Published by AuthorHouse 06/06/2019

ISBN: 978-1-7283-1462-4 (sc)
ISBN: 978-1-7283-1461-7 (e)

Approval

Analyzing the Fair Market Value of Assets and
the Stakeholders' Investment Decisions
by

Anis I. Milad

Approved by:

Dr. Glenn H. Walton   7/21/08

Chair: *Glenn H. Walton, PhD*   Date

Members: *Rocky J. Dwyer, PhD*
              Shirley E. Johnson, PhD

Certified by:

Freda Turner   7/29/08

School Dean: *Freda mer, PhD*   Date

Abstract

Analyzing the Fair Market Value of Assets and
the Stakeholders' Investment Decisions
by

Anis I. Milad

Northcentral University, July 2008

This dissertation was designed to investigate the relationship between the fair market value of assets and stakeholders' investment decisions. The Financial Accounting Standard Board (FASB) is primarily responsible for establishing Generally Accepted Accounting Principles (GAAP) (Weygandt, Kieso, & Kimmel, 2003). According to the FASB, GAAP require disclosing the fair value of assets of organizations. This research investigated the effect of the disclosure of fair value of assets on stakeholders' investment decisions.

The research question was: How does the hidden market value of assets affect male and female stakeholders' investment decisions? The survey positively answered this question. Both female and male respondents (519) agreed the market value of assets helps them make better investment decisions. The participants equally shared the need to know the current market value of the company's assets to make better investment decisions. The investment decisions were shared evenly by the female and male participants.

Acknowledgements

I would like to thank the Dissertation Committee, Dr. Glenn Walton (chairperson), Dr. Rocky Dwyer (member), Dr. Shirley Johnson (member), Dr. Ann Nelson (external reviewer) for their mentorship, guidance, and patience. Special thanks to my Academic Advisor Ms. Jennifer Benacci for her excellent communication skill, and Dr. Diane Dusick and her team for editing my paper. I also would like to thank my wife and best friend, Lauren, for her support'and understanding. Finally, I dedicate this degree to my parents.

Contents

List of Table

List of Figures

Chapter 1

INTRODUCTION

The Financial Accounting Standard Board (FASB) is primarily responsible for establishing Generally Accepted Accounting Principles (GAAP) (Weygandt, Kieso, & Kimmel, 2003). According to the FASB, GAAP require disclosing the fair value of assets of organizations. This research investigated the effects of the disclosure of fair value of assets on stakeholders' investment decisions.

Assets are recorded on balance sheets in accordance with the historical cost, which is the purchase price of an asset. During the estimated useful life of assets, the market value of plant assets often exceeds the historical costs of those assets on the balance sheet. Users of financial statements are not aware of the current fair market value of the assets of a corporation. In the 1990s, fair value balance sheets and income statements based on the fair value of assets began to be used in Europe and other parts of the world (e.g., Australia and United Kingdom), reflecting investors' request that corporations reveal the true value of their assets and liabilities (Ernst & Young, 2005).

The appreciation of assets is the manifestation of the market forces that affect the assets' value (Chen & Wei, 1993). Investors might wish to know the fair value of assets of companies in order to realistically evaluate their investments (Ernst & Young, 2005). Historical cost-based financial statements are questionable statements that do not reveal the actual financial position of a company because historical cost accounting was a recording system for economic events that occurred at one moment in time (Weygandt et al., 2003). According to Cole (2004), the practice of historical cost accounting could be referred to as evidence of frozen principles in a dynamic market context.

Statement of the Problem

Financial statements are based on historical costs, and the omission of the market value of assets is a deceiving practice because the market value of the assets is not reflected on financial statements (Miller & Loftus, 2000). Accordingly, the balance sheet, which is based on historical costs, is not a true *snapshot* of a company's current financial position (Ernst & Young, 2005). Furthermore, the manifestation of the appreciation of assets is *hidden power* for corporate leaders because it permits an increase in the cash that is reinvested in the company, and it is not recorded on the financial statements. It is not clear whether there is a relationship between the market value of assets and stakeholders' investment decisions.

Although the appreciation of assets might affect the stakeholders' decisions, the historical costs principle of accounting has been used to record the financial position of organizations. Financial statements reflect both the historical costs of the assets and the market prices of securities. Market prices are routinely reported in the securities section of the financial statements. For example, the inventory valuation, Lower of Cost or Market and Last in First out (LIFO), and the investment valuation, available-for-sales securities are valuations based on market prices (Kieso, Weygandt, & Warfield, 2007).

Treasury stock is bought and resold using market prices. Common stock and preferred stock are sold above par and are paid in capital of excess of par value used to record gains or losses. Investments in other companies' stocks (e.g., available-for-sale security) are recorded under current assets at fair value, and the unrealized gain is recorded in the stockholders' equity. The inconsistency in the recording of assets and equity on balance sheets and expense accounts, including depreciation on the income statement, were the subject of the current research.

The GMP emphasize the cost principles for recording the cost of assets (Weygandt et al., 2003). The GMP further require the allocation of assets' historical cost during the useful life of the assets. Buying a building in Manhattan is a growth investment and also an increase in the market value as well as income investment (Benston & Wall, 2005).

Real estate and securities investment are both assets (Weygandt et al., 2003). Listings of common shares above the par value is recorded and documented. Losses and gains of short-term investments are recorded on financial statements as documentation for the market value of the securities during the life of the securities. Conversely, the current value of a building that has appreciated is economic power and a source of hidden wealth; but it is not recorded. Not recording the appreciated value of a building is both an ethical and a financial dilemma because the current value of assets is significant and should not be ignored (Ernst & Young, 2005).

Background and Significance of the Problem

When an individual borrows money using the equity of a certain asset, the loan is considered a liability. The recorded historical cost of the asset is not affected by the new transaction. The equity portion of the asset is not recorded because it is considered market value of the asset, and the GAAP request companies record only the historical cost of assets (Weygandt et al., 2003).

According to Bloom, Weimer, and Fisher (1982), companies have the power to borrow money using the current value of assets as collateral, but there are no changes to the historical costs of the assets on the balance sheet. If the company does not mortgage the asset, the equity portion is never recorded, yet it is considered hidden economic power and unused wealth. When the mortgage is paid off, the historical cost of the asset remains unchanged; but the market value of the asset generally continues to rise. Borrowing is based on the current market value of an asset, and cash is obtained through borrowing. If the current market value is removed from the equation, borrowing is not possible (Bloom et al., 1982).

Demanding the fair value of assets to be recorded instead of the historical costs challenges cost principles accounting (Cole, 2004). Recording assets with their historical costs creates the illusion of an accurate financial position, and it deceives investors and creditors. If the fair value of assets were recorded, the economy would evolve into a new era because companies would record their true value (Cole, 2004).

The Chief Accountant of the U.S. Securities and Exchange Commission (SEC), Lynn E. Turner, wrote a letter to Arlene Thomas, Vice President of the American Institute of Certified Public Accountants (AICPA), requesting that the AICPA provide industry guidance on models and methodologies for valuation (Turner, 2000). According to Turner's letter in today's dynamic economy, financial statement users have become increasingly interested in the fair value of a company's assets and liabilities, in addition to the historical cost information already provided in the financial statements.

Research Question

One research question guided the current study: How does the hidden market value of assets affect male and female stakeholders' investment decisions?

Brief Review of Related Literature

The purpose of the current study was to investigate the influence of the fair market value of assets on stakeholders' decisions. Previous researchers (Chen & Wei, 1993; Cole, 2004; Devine, 2002; Gonedes, 1981; Haddad, Nathur, Rangan, & Tadisina, 1993; Horngren & Harrison, 1989; Kempner, 2002; Larson, Wild, & Chiappetta, 2005; Lee, Press, & Choi, 2001; MacDonald & Richardson, 2002; McNichols, 1954; Mosich & Larsen, 1982; Ro, 1981) have investigated the fair value of assets as a concept and recommended that the fair value of assets be used instead of the historical cost principle of accounting in financial statements.

The focus of the current research was to investigate the effect of the fair value of assets on stakeholders in light of the recent statements of GAAP, which require the disclosure of the fair value of assets of organizations. Theoretical evidence has supported the influence of the fair value financial statements on stakeholders (Cole, 2004; Devine, 2002). The distinctive contribution of the current research was the statistical analysis of data obtained from a sample of participants who favor or disfavor fair value financial statements, a practice that would uncover their company's potential economic power produced by the appreciation of assets.

Definition of Key Tenns

The following terms and phrases are defined as they were used in the current study:

Appreciation value. Appreciation is an increase in value (Siegel & Shim, 2005).

Assets appreciated value. Assets appreciated value refers to an increase in the value of assets (Siegel & Shim, 2005).

Depreciation expense. Depreciation is the process of spreading the original cost of an asset over the estimated life of the fixed asset (e.g. building, equipment) (Siegel & Shim, 2005).

Economic events. Economic events are business transactions requiring a journal entry.

Fair market value. Fair market value refers to the amount that could be received on the sale of an asset (Siegel & Shim, 2005).

Historical cost of the asset. The original cost of an asset, ignoring inflationary increases, is referred to as historical cost of the asset (Siegel & Shim, 2005).

Market Capitalization: Outstanding shares X Market price per share. Legal capital. The par-value issued stock or the stated value of no par issued stock is the legal capital (Siegel & Shim, 2005).

Price-earnings ratio. Price-earnings ratios equal the market price per share divided by the earning per share (Siegel & Shim, 2005).

Retained earnings. Retained earnings are accumulated earnings of a corporation since inception less dividends (Siegel & Shim, 2005).

Straight-line depreciation. Straight-line depreciation is a method providing equal depreciation charges for each period.

Limitations of the Study

The survey conducted in this research, was administered via the Internet. There were significant advantages to using the Internet to conduct the survey and recruit participants. The data collection instrument reached a large number of potential participants with relative ease (Bordens & Abbott,

2002). Also the survey provided a quick, inexpensive, efficient, and accurate means of assessing information about a population (Trochim, 2001). However, the limitation of this survey was the population, which included only students who were well educated at Northcentral University.

Chapter 2

REVIEW OF LITERATURE

Earnings and the Usefulness of Accounting Information

Earnings and stock returns. Although ambiguity in the return/earnings relationship can contribute to a weak association between earnings and stock returns, there is a strong possibility that the tow quality of reported earnings causes this ambiguity (Lev, 1990). Messages (e.g., financial reports or news broadcasts) convey information if they cause a change in the receiver's probability distribution (i.e., beliefs). Such a change in the probability distribution triggers an action; and if an action reflected by a change in stock price or volume, for example, can be attributed to specific information, such information is considered useful. This is the logic underlying the returns/earnings association studies (Lev, 1990).

Investors look for solid, useful information (Ernst & Young, 2005). Reported earnings are confusing because the reality of the appreciated assets and the appreciation value allocation is ignored in the recent accounting principles issued by the GAAP. The appreciated value of an asset is useful information that should contribute to the logic underlying the returns/earning association (Lev, 1990).

Misinterpreting the implication for future profitability. Investors can misinterpret the implications for future profitability of growth in long term net operating assets because this growth has a weaker association with future profitability than current aggregate earnings (Fairfield, Whisenant, & Yohn, 2003). Even notes on financial statements are misleading. For example, current accounting regulations do not mandate the disclosure of all covenant violations (Chen & Wei, 1993). In the current system, the growth of net operating assets has a weaker association with future probability, which demands the change of the allocation of historical costs. These allocations can mislead investors because the notes to financial statements do not completely disclose violations and the lack of reasonable valuation of the assets (Chen & Wei, 1993).

Earnings announcements and stock prices. Two measures of change are typically correlated; (a) change in the stock price (i.e., return) around the earnings announcement and (b) the change in the firm's equity (i.e., earnings). Given that stock prices reflect expectations about future earnings before the earnings are announced, it is reasonable to correlate the change in price (i.e., return) with unexpected earnings (i.e., new information) rather than with reported earnings. This procedure can increase the power of the return/earnings analysis (Lev, 1990). Nevertheless, unexpected earnings at the time of announcement might convey only a small part of the total information in earnings (Lev, 1990).

Lev (1990) noted the importance of the correlation between stock prices and a firm's future earnings before such earnings are announced. Accordingly, the allocation of the appreciation value of assets should be taken into consideration because of its effect on earnings, which in turn affect stock prices. Stock prices directly affect a firm's earnings and indirectly affect stock prices.

There are three suggested ways to calculate the appreciated value of an asset. The first approach is to divide the total amount of the future value of the asset by its useful life in years, using the future value of a single amount (Brigham & Gapenski, 1994). The second approach is to estimate the periodical allocations (i.e., installments) of each year of the useful life of the asset, using the future value of annuity (Brigham & Gapenski, 1994).

The third approach is to calculate the appreciated value of an asset using a new depreciation method discussed in this proposal as a new alternative. Because the assets are recorded at their fair values in the third approach, the practice will increase or decrease the net worth of the company. It is impossible to calculate net worth if the assets are recorded at historical costs because the net worth is the total value of all possessions (Downes & Goodman, 2006).

The market's reaction to regulatory accounting events. The market's reaction to regulatory accounting events and the reported findings have been inconsistent because of the confounding of events and results (Haddad et al., 1993). The inconsistencies in the accounting principles, regulatory accounting events, and application of principles have been reflected in the inconsistent real estate taxes. These taxes have been based on the ongoing market value of assets and have required the depreciation of the same assets to be based on the historical costs (Haddad et al., 1993).

Haddad et al. (1993) and Lev, 1990, for example have examined and tested the market reaction to regulatory accounting events. Accounting events are sometimes confounding, and different researchers have arrived at different conclusions for the same event. For example, earnings persistence is defined as the extent to which an innovation (i.e., unexpectedness) in the earnings series causes investors to revise their expectations about future earnings (lev, 1990). Unexpectedness in earnings is not the only reason investors revise their expectations about future earnings. Speculating the fair value of assets could be a major reason for investors to revise their expectations about future earnings (lev, 1990).

Appreciation

Appreciation (i.e., growth as increase in value) of assets involves the historical cost of assets, inflation, and replacement costs (Siegel & Shim, 2005). Depreciation costs have been discussed in the accounting literature.

Devine (2002) argued the historical cost of an asset led to an historical depreciation cost that overstates the net income.

It is crucial to look into the future and to estimate not only the life of an asset but also its expected replacement cost when replacement costs become necessary (Devine, 2002). The financing of replacements and of depreciation funds should not be separated. Conversely, Kempner (2002) stated scholars should not confuse depreciation with the financing of replacements.

Depreciation, which is based on historical costs for appreciated assets, does not reflect the relationship between the growth of assets and the allocation of the appreciation value of those assets (Siegel & Shim, 2005). Historicalcost accounting indicates the appreciation value of assets is frozen in time, but the fact dictates assets (e.g., buildings) have appreciated or depreciated, and the value of the assets is changing. If a building is used for commercialpurposes, normally the rent revenues increase steadily year after year during the useful life of the assets.

The matching principles and the increase in revenue will not match the depreciation expense that does not increase. Expenses (e.g., utilities, rent, and advertising) are all recorded based upon market prices, except for the depreciation expense, which is based on the historical cost. For example, utility companies' charges are based on the market price of energy.

Inflation, Replacement Cost, and Growth

Inflation. Inflation is an essential element to consider when determining the depreciation cost and the appreciation (i.e., growth) of an asset. Historical cost depreciation tends to overstate earnings because of inflation effects, which in tum misrepresent the firms' capacities to expand operations or to distribute dividends (Lee et al., 2001). King (2003) suggested, in a period of zero or even low inflation, values tend to decline, but inflation tends to increase the value of an asset.

Increases in prices in the marketplace are based on demand and supply of goods, tangible assets, and intangible assets, as well as on inflation, which contributes to the increase in prices in general. The values of assets decline in a period of low inflation and increase in periods of high inflation. Practically, if depreciation is based on historical cost, earnings are overstated because of the inflation effects and other elements such as pricing and politics (Howe & Harvey, 1987; Vickman, 1986).

Replacement cost. Measuring current and replacement costs of assets is possible, but scholars have expressed skepticism, making cautious suggestions regarding departure from historic cost principles (Kempner, 2002). Kempner noted there were no adequate means to measure cost dollars with current ones. Devine (2002) remarked there were difficulties with estimating replacement costs years in advance.

According to GAAP, when an asset is placed in service, the asset is to be utilized fully during its useful life, and the money should be used to replace the old asset. The unique idea in the current study was to include the replacement costs of assets in the legal capital, which is the amount of the par value of the issued stock of an organization. It is not logical *to* designate the legal capital for creditors and not consider the replacement costs as capital reseNed for the on-going success of a company.

Organizational leaders may or may not replace the depreciated asset at the end of its useful life; but the current value of a new asset will be close *to* the replacement costs, in case the organizational leaders set aside the periodic depreciation expense as a result of the appreciation of the asset. The replacement costs will lead to a new recording process that guarantees the money will be there to replace the asset. Depreciation expense, which is based on the appreciation value of the asset, is also a replacement cost reserve, and should not be added to the statement of cash flow (Weygandt et al., 2003).

Depreciation and replacement costs. The definition of depreciation is not narrow and applies to all types of assets. "Depreciation may be defined as that inevitable disappearance of the value of certain items of physical property which can normally be expected in the course of the conduct of the business enterprises" (Mason, 2002, p. 106). Assets such as buildings should be treated differently from all other assets such as equipment and machines. Buildings depreciate or appreciate in value. The depreciation/appreciation costs of a building are affected by the market's demand/supply, growth/reduction, inflation/deflation, and historical/replacement costs. Stating assets can be construed as a prepaid expense (Kempner, 2002) reflects a limited point of view.

If depreciation were to be a periodic charge against revenue for the service of a plant, it would appear more equitable to base depreciation upon the original prepaid expense. Depreciation/appreciation would refer strictly to the historical cost of the asset (Kempner, 2002). The definition of depreciation is consistent with attempts to calculate depreciation expenses based on the appreciation value of an asset. During the useful life of the asset, the asset might increase or decrease in value; but the status of the asset after the expiration of the useful life depends on the market value and level of deterioration of the asset (Siegel & Shim, 2005}. The replacement cost should be used based on the fair market value of the asset, whether the management would replace the asset, demolish it, or to sell it to acquire a new one.

Historical Cost and Change in Prices

Net income and misrepresentation. In general, the consequences of adopting the historical cost of an asset are (a} the overstating of net income, and (b) misleading the users of financial statements (Cole, 2004). If net income is overstated as a result of miscalculating depreciation, the income statement will not include a proper amount for depreciation in its costs. Overstating net income leads to misinterpretation in that either the surplus is exaggerated or dividends have to be paid from retained earnings out of unearned income. Retained earnings account is the accumulation of net income/loss.

Stockholders will believe their securities are worth more than they really are, investors might buy stock under a similar misapprehension, and forecasters are likely to be misled (Cole, 2004). Using the historical cost of an asset can have a domino effect. The net income is overstated, the dividends are paid from unearned income, the income before income taxes is inflated, the income taxes are overstated, investors are misled into believing the securities are worth more than they really are, and earnings per share are overstated, inflating the price-earnings ratio (Cole, 2004).

In the depreciation method this paper proposes, the expectation is the income before income taxes will be reduced because the depreciation, which is calculated according to the assets' appreciated value, will be much higher than the depreciation based on the historical cost of the assets. Accordingly, the income to be taxed will be reduced (Cole, 2004). This dissertation was based on the assumption that the cost principles are inconsistent because one asset, such as a building, has been calculated using the historical cost of the asset and another asset such as an available-for-sale security, has been calculated using the fair market value of the asset. Earnings-per-share, however, will be affected by the depreciation expense of the increased/decreased value of the assets.

Traditional calculation. The traditional calculation of the depreciation methods (e.g., straight-line) of an asset is problematic. Nielsen (2002) proposed an accounting principle in which errors also result under the straight-line method because the service lives of assets cannot be predicted with exactness. The inference is the historical costs methodology is the wrong alternative for appreciable assets.

Based upon evidence, Ro (1981) concluded the disclosure of the replacement costs (RC) accounting data, as required by the SEC, had no effect on the volume of common stock shares traded for the firms affected by the new disclosure requirement. Nevertheless, evidence from the literature does not imply depreciation, which is based on the appreciation of assets, does not play a role in investors' decisions when the RC is driven by the appreciation of assets. The ethical issue concerns the fact that the use of historical cost depreciation leads to overstating earnings, which is a misrepresentation of firms' capacities to expand operations or to distribute dividends (Lee et al., 2001). Using the historical cost of an asset is an ethical dilemma because investors do not realize depreciation, which is based on the historical cost of an asset, leads to overstatements of earnings.

Errors associated with historical cost depreciation. McNichols (1954) argued accounting should reflect the changes in the value of assets and the historical cost should remain separate. Current researchers have argued one of the most important and controversial factors associated with adjustment for price-level change of the assets have been the problem of how to reflect adjustments in accounting books (Lee et al., 2001). It is essential to retain historical cost records and, at the same time, to record the changes in assets' accounts due to the fluctuating dollar (McNichols, 1954).

Lee et al. (2001) suggested financial statements fell short in accurately reflecting the costs of employing capital assets. The trend in overstating earnings, excluding the effects of inflation, misrepresents the ability of a firm to distribute dividends or expand operations. A firm's capital structures can be a factor in earnings measurement errors associated with historical cost depreciation. Overstated earnings cause earnings measurement errors that are associated with historical cost depreciation (Lee et at., 2001).

Fair Value Measurements

Changes in fair value. Fair value measurements of assets, liabilities, and components of equity can arise from both the initial recording of transactions and later changes in value. Changes in fair value measurements that occur over time may be treated in different ways under GAAP. For example, GAAP may require some fair value changes be reflected in net income whereas other fair value changes may be reflected in other comprehensive income and equity (Anonymous, 2003).

While Statement SAS No. 101 provides guidance on auditing fair value measurements and disclosures, evidence obtained from other audit procedures also provide evidence relevant to the measurement and disclosure of fair values. For example, inspection procedures that verify the existence of an asset measured at fair value can provide relevant evidence about its valuation such as the physical condition of the asset (Anonymous, 2003). Auditors should obtain sufficient competent audit evidence to provide reasonable assurance that fair value measurements and disclosures confonn with the GAA.P. The GAA.P require certain items be measured at fair value.

According to Anonymous (2003),

The Financial Accounting Standards Board (FASB) Statement of Financial Accounting Concepts No. 7, *Using Cash Flow Information and Present Value in Accounting Measurements,* defines the fair value of an asset (or liability) as the amount at which that asset (or liability) could be bought (or incurred) or sold (or settled) in a current transaction between willing parties, that is, other than in a forced or liquidation sale.

Although the GAAP may not prescribe the method for measuring the fair value of an item, it expresses a preference for the use of observable market prices to make that determination. In the absence of observable market prices, the GAAP require the fair value to be based on the best information available in the circumstances.

Management is responsible for making the fair value measurements and disclosures included in the financial statements. As part of fulfilling its responsibility, management needs to establish an accounting and financial reporting process for determining the fair value measurements and disclosures, select appropriate valuation methods, identify and adequately support any significant assumptions used, prepare the valuation, and ensure that the presentation and disclosure of the fair value measurements are in accordance with the GAAP. ('If 3-4)

Values-relevant information. In settings with realistic market assumptions, fair value is not well-defined because it needs to be defined and adopted by GAAP. These results in three value constructs: (a) entry values, (b) exit values, and (c) value-in-use. Because these types of values are unobservable, implementation of fair value accounting requires their estimation, potentially introducing estimation error. Unless estimation error is severe, value-in-use is the appropriate construct for firm valuation because it captures the total firm value associated with an asset (Barth & Landsman, 1995).

Neither the balance sheet nor the income statement fully reflects all of the value-relevant information because it is based on historical costs. Income realization can be potentially valuation-relevant, although management discretion can detract from its relevance. Barth and Landsman (1995) maintained there was no basis for recognizing income, only realized gains and losses; and for this reason, the concept of core earnings and fair value accounting are unrelated.

According to Barth and Landsman (1995), in the more realistic setting of imperfect and incomplete markets, there are six key issues. First, fair value is not well-defined because entry and exit values and value-in-use can differ. Second, because each of the three value constructs may be unobservable, implementation of fair value accounting requires their estimation, introducing the potential for measurement error. Third, one primary difference between value-in-use and the other two constructs relates to the intangible value of management skills.

Fourth, fair value accounting should focus on value-in-use because it is the only measure that always captures total firm value associated with an asset and is consistent with the going concern tenet of the GAAP. Fifth, separate disclosure of the components of value-in-use is potentially informative in the presence of measurement error. Finally, separate disclosure of realized and unrealized gains and losses can provide information about asset fair values that otherwise would be unavailable if only the total were disclosed although there is information loss in the presence of measurement error and when managers selectively realize gains and losses (Barth & Landsman, 1995).

Benston and Wall (2005) suggested present accounting principles were largely based on a system that values assets and liabilities at their historic costs rather than at their current market values. Historic-cost accounting reflects an emphasis on providing reliable financial information even if the information is not the most relevant to the problem facing the decision maker. The FASB's move toward use of fair-value accounting, particularly for financial instruments, reflects the belief that fair values could and would be measured with sufficient reliability by managers and could be audited effectively by independent public accountants (Benston & Wall, 2005).

Consequently, fair value would provide more relevant information to decision makers. The concepts of relevance and reliability as expressed by the FASB show how the present GAAP has systematically selected options that have greater reliability at the expense of relevance (Benston & Wall, 2005). The next section is a discussion of the issues raised by the FASB's proposed move to fair-value accounting.

Move to fair-value accounting. The FASB's interest in implementing fair-value accounting for financial instruments was dated to at least 1991, with *FAS 107, Disclosures about Fair Value* of *Financial Instruments* (as cited Benston & Wall, 2005). FAS 115, *Accounting for Certain Investments in Debt and Equity Securities* (as cited Benston & Wall, 2005) required the inclusion of fair values in balance sheets and income statements. This reduced the practice of only including disclosure in footnotes for securities not held to maturity and for which reliable market prices could be determined by reference to securities regularly traded on recognized securities exchanges (Benston & Wall, 2005).

Benston and Wall (2005) stated,

FAS 133, Accounting for Derivative Instruments and Hedging Activity (enacted in 1998), expressed the FASB view forcefully: Fair value is the most relevant measure for financial instruments, and the only relevant measure for derivative instruments. The primary benefit of fair-value accounting, according to the FASB, is discussed in its Preliminary Views: The major conceptual advantage of fair value as a measurement attribute is that, because it is a market-based notion, it is unaffected by (a) the history of the asset or liability, that is, fair value does not depend on the date or cost at which an asset or liability is acquired or incurred; (b) the specific entity that holds the asset or owns the liability, that is, fair value is the same no matter which entity has an asset or liability (if both entities have access to the same markets and, for a liability, if they have the same credit standing); and (c) the future of the asset or liability that is fair value does not depend on the intended disposition of an asset or liability. (1J 36).

The fair value of assets is measured as a value in exchange, the amounts for which an asset can be sold, or a liability extinguished. These exit values necessarily understate the values to investors in companies that do not expect to dispose of their assets. For what companies refer to as *going* concerns, the value of assets is value-in-use (i.e. present values). If assets could be sold for more than their value-in-use, they should and usually would be sold. Assets that are kept would almost always have greater values in use than in exchange. Fair values understate the economic value of those assets to the owners of an enterprise (Benston & Wall, 2005).

Financial institution. Black (1997) noted the banking industry, like other industries, had reported its financial condition and results of operations on the basis of historical cost accounting. Historical cost accounting is based on the fundamental premise that the cost of the item will be fully recovered. Consequently, changes in fair value or market value are irrelevant. Under historical cost accounting, assets and liabilities are reported at their original cost in the statement of financial condition. Subsequent changes in the value of a particular asset or liability caused by changing market conditions after the original transaction date are usually not recognized (Black, 1997)

According to Black (1997) in financial institutions, the cost of an item was usually represented by the cash proceeds that changed hands at the time of an original event or transaction. This cost is reported as the basis of the event or transaction; the subsequent income-related effect of the transaction or event continues to reflect the historical cost basis. Other gains and losses from the event or transaction are not reported until management decides to exit its position in the transaction, sell the related assetor repay the acquired liability.

Exposure draft. Botosan et al. (2005) stated the FASB Exposure

Draft (ED) proposed procedural guidance for measuring most fair value estimates required by other authoritative accounting pronouncements. This guidance would apply broadly to financial and nonfinancial assets and liabilities. The ED also proposed expanded footnote disclosure concerning the methods and inputs used to determine fair value estimates. These disclosures were intended to assist financial statement users in assessing the reliability of fair value estimates reported in the primary financial statements (Botosan et al., 2005). The committee supported the formulation of a single standard that provides guidance on fair value measurement. It is believed such a standard would improve the consistency of fair value measurement across the many standards that require value reporting and disclosure (Botosan et al., 2005).

According to Botosan et al. (2005) two important factors contributed to the perceived need for the general guidance on fair value measurement proposed in the ED. First, the current set of accounting standards included no single source of generally applicable guidance for defining and estimating fair value. Instead, fair value measurement guidance was primarily contained in a cross-referenced patchwork of accounting standards related to financial instruments.

The ED proposed a single standard to guide all fair value estimates. Second, recent accounting standards reflected increasing acceptance of fair value as a measurement attribute as compared to amortized cost (Botosan et al., 2005). Given the high likelihood future accounting standards will incorporate fair value measurements, defining the fair value measurement attribute, along with high-levelprocedural guidance for consistent estimation of that attribute, becomes increasingly important for the efficient application of new and existing accounting standards (Botosan et al., 2005).

Botosan et al. (2005) found a considerable body of research examining the relevance and reliability of fair value estimates derived from various sources. The majority of these studies assessed whether fair value disclosures for financial instruments were associated with share prices. The studies were based on the assumption that, if the fair values of firms' net assets are relevant to investors and are reliably measured, the amounts will be positively related to share prices. In terms of statistical analysis coefficients on assets or liabilities will be positive or negative when the share price is regressed on fair value information and relevant control variables (Botosan et al., 2005).

The literature generally indicated fair values obtained from actively traded markets were more reliably associated with share prices than fair value estimates derived from thinly-traded markets or internal estimation models. For example, research on banks and property-casualty insurers showed fair values for equity investments and U.S. Treasury securities were related to share prices, but fair values for investments with less readily available market prices (e.g., corporate and municipal bonds) were not (Botosan et al., 2005). Using a sample of closed-end mutual funds, Botosan et al. found a strong statistical association between share prices and fair values for investment securities traded in thin markets. The authors attributed the differences in their results to the fact that the net assets of closed-end mutual funds consisted entirely of financial instruments reported at fair value (Botosan et al., 2005).

Valuation of assets/properties. Regarding the valuation of Assets/ Properties, the U.S. GAAP require properties, plants, and equipment be recorded in the financial statements based upon their historical costs and allow permanent decreases in the value to be expensed. International Accounting Standards (lAS) requires the initial recording based upon actual costs, but allow revaluation of assets using their fair values in future years. The valuation of assets based on their fair values has been debated in the United States and in foreign countries for a long time.

Proponents have argued fair values provided updated information that could be used to analyze financial statements and make decisions whereas historical values were less relevant (Chawla, 2003). Critics have argued it was difficult to determine fair values unless assets were actually sold in the market (Chawla, 2003). Critics further argued the valuation process is a result of subjective judgments made by appraisers and do not provide objective hard numbers as is the case with historical values. Moreover, there is room for manipulation of fair values because of subjective judgments, but historical values are not open to such manipulation. Overall, historical values appear to be more reliable because they provide actual costs incurred to acquire assets (Chawla, 2003).

The FASB recently issued the exposure draft of a proposed Statement of Financial Accounting Standards (FAS), to provide guidance for how to measure fair value. The proposed FAS defines *fair value* as the price at which an asset or liability could be exchanged in a current transaction between knowledgeable, unrelated, willing parties. In the proposed FAS, the FASB presumed a willing party to be a marketplace participant representing an unrelated buyer and an unrelated seller who are knowledgeable, have a common level of understanding about factors relevant to the asset or liability and the transaction, and are willing and able to transact in the same market with the legal and financial ability to do so. The proposed FAS also clarified the objective of a fair-value measurement, which is to estimate an exchange price for the asset or liability being measured in the absence of an actual transaction for that asset or liability (Eiifoglu & Fitzsimons, 2004).

The proposed FAS clarified the objective of a fair-value measurement, which is to estimate an exchange price for the asset or liability being measured in the absence of an actual transaction for that asset or liability. For a liability, the proposed FAS would provide that the estimate of fair value consider the effect of the entity's credit standing so the estimate reflects the amount that would be observed in an exchange between willing parties of the same credit quality. In such situations, the estimate would be determined by reference to a current hypothetical transaction between willing parties (Eiifoglu & Fitzsimons, 2004).

The proposed FAS would create a fair-value hierarchy that would group the inputs to be used to estimate fair value into three broad categories or levels. The hierarchy would give highest priority to market inputs that reflect quoted prices in active markets for identical assets and liabilities whether those prices are quoted in terms of completed transaction prices, bid-and-asked prices, or rates. The FASB would give the lowest priority to entity inputs developed based on an entity's internal estimates and assumptions (Eiifoglu & Fitzsimons, 2004). Elifoglu and Fitzsimons noted the fair-value levels that would be used to estimate fair value:

Level 1 Estimates: The FASB noted that fair value would be estimated using quoted prices for identical assets or liabilities in active reference markets whenever that information is available. Furthermore, quoted prices used for a Level 1 estimate would not be adjusted.

Level 2 Estimates: The proposed FAS would require that, if quoted prices for identicalassets or liabilities in active markets were not available, fair value would be estimated using quoted prices for similar assets or liabilities in active markets, adjusted as appropriate for differences, whenever that information is available.

Level 3 Estimates: The proposed FAS would require that, if quoted prices for identical or similar assets or liabilities in active markets were not available or if differences between similar assets or liabilities were not objectively determinable, the fair value be estimated using multiple valuation techniques consistent with the market approach, income approach, and cost approach, whenever the information necessary to apply those techniques is available without undue cost and effort (Eiifoglu & Fitzsimons, 2004).

Exposure draft (ED) in Australia. According to Fargher (2001), accounting for all financial instruments at fair value is a controversial practice strongly opposed by banking groups and is currently under review by standard setters. In Australia, opposition to ED Financial Instruments, including opposition from the banking industry, resulted in an accounting standard (i.e., AASB 1033, Presentation and Disclosure of Financial Instruments) that is limited to requiring disclosure of the fair values of derivative securities. The issue of recognition of gains and losses was deferred. The need to align with lAS will ensure fair-value accounting for financial instruments will again become an issue for Australian standard setters (Fargher, (2001).

The variables in Fargher's (2001) study were summarized by three characteristic variables that could potentially influence the results. The variables were (a) firm size, (b) the nature of the firm's activities, and (c) whether the firm was a foreign entity. The levelof support for fair-value accounting was measured using a five-point Likert-type scale. Respondents were asked one question: "Do you support the concept of marking all financial assets and liabilities, including derivatives and non-trading transactions in 'banking books,' to fair value on the balance sheet with movements in fair value reflected in the profit and loss?" The five-point

Likert-type scale was converted to a numeric scale coded as 1 *(strongly oppose)* to 5 *(strongly support).* This variable was treated as a dichotomous variable measuring support or opposition for the purposes of a logistic regression. Fargher's study found respondents who supported fair value accounting for all financial instruments did not tend to agree with the statement that fair value will cause volatility in earnings unrelated to economic activity.

Conversion to fair value. Although progress has been made in making financial statements more relevant by the inclusion of current value information, the piecemeal standard-by-standard approach has resulted in a lack of consistency in the specification of valuation bases. At the international level, there has been disagreement between standard setters on a unifying concept, with advocates of value-to-the-entity and advocates of fair-value. No solution has been provided by the FASB's departure and rejection of entity-specific valuation. The mixed measurement system raises questions about reporting on financial performance (Miller & Loftus, 2000).

Conversion to fair value generates credits and debits that cannot be hidden in the balance sheet and allowed to masquerade as assets and liabilities under the conceptualframeworks in the United States, the United Kingdom, and Australia. The piecemeal approach in building the mixed measurement system has resulted in inconsistent treatment of valuation adjustments. The lAS Committee has a high-level steering committee addressing the key issues related to financial performance, yet it is unclear whether the committee can facilitate the progressive swing to current value by providing a sensible framework within which to report value changes (Miller & Loftus, 2000). To date, the FASB has provided no solution for implementing the fair value of assets in financialreporting.

Relevance and reliability. The debate on fair-value accounting has revolved around the issues of relevance and reliability. Before discussing the issues of relevance of fair value, it is important to review how fair value and relevance are generally defined.

Fair value is defined in the FASB's Preliminary Views document as an estimate of the price an entity would have realized if it had sold an asset or paid, if it had been relieved of a liability on the reporting date in an arm's-length exchange motivated by normal business considerations. (Poon, 2004, 1f 2)

Poon further explained, "Relevance is defined as the capacity of information to make a difference in a decision by helping users form predictions about the outcomes of past, present, and future events, or to confirm or correct expectations" (1(2).

Fair values reflect the effects of current market conditions, and changes in fair values reflect the effects of changes in market conditions when they take place (Poon, 2004). In contrast, historical cost information reflects only the effects of conditions that existed when the transaction took place, and the effects of price changes are reflected only when they are realized. As fair values incorporate current information about current market conditions and expectations, they are expected to provide a superior basis for prediction to outdated cost figures because these outdated cost figures reflect outdated market conditions and expectations (Poon, 2004).

Although most researchers have agreed fair values were the most relevant measure for financial assets and liabilities an entity actively trades, some scholars, most notably in the banking industry, have argued historical cost was the more appropriate measure if management intended to hold an asset or to owe a liability until maturity. The rationale for accounting on an historical cost basis is it better reflects the economic substance of transactions and actual cash flow over time. Conversely, fair value information would reflect the effects of transactions and events in which the entity would not participate therefore would often be irrelevant. The question is whether management's decision to hold assets or to continue to owe liabilities in light of changed market conditions is relevant in evaluating the entity's financial position and performance (Poon, 2004).

Conclusions

The importance of depreciation in accounting has been well documented in the literature, and many findings have supported the use of straight-line depreciation because it produces a smoother earnings stream than accelerated depreciation. The smoothing effect can be realized without changes in accounting policy. However, Barefield and Comiskey (1971) found the rate of growth in earnings to be higher under an accelerated policy than under straight-line depreciation.

If changing the depreciation method from a straight-line method of depreciation to an accelerated depreciation method results in a higher growth in earnings, the comparison between the use of historical cost and the use of the appreciation value of assets to calculate depreciation should be addressed and investigated. According to previous literature, as prices rise, the real value of depreciation based on historic costs decreases.

A company's taxable income increases faster than it would if depreciation reflected the actual replacement costs (Gonedes, 1981).

Changes in depreciation methods can change the levels of earnings. When a firm reserves the replacement cost based on the depreciation of the ongoing value of an asset, the firm's taxable income decreases and eliminates the inconsistency of the current accounting principles. Depreciation, which is based on historical costs for appreciated assets, does not reflect the relationship between the growth of assets and the allocation of the appreciation value of assets (Siegel & Shim, 2005). The historical cost accounting method records the appreciation value of assets frozen in time, but assets (e.g., buildings) appreciate, and the value of the assets changes.

Chapter 3

METHODOLOGY

Overview

The current study was conducted with a quantitative research design to examine how the hidden market value of assets affects stakeholders. Correlational analyses were conducted to examine relationships among variables and to test hypotheses (Zikmund, 2003). Independent -samples *t* test were used to investigate the two independent groups, female participants and male participants (SPSS, 2005; Zikmund, 2003).

Restatement of Problem

Financial statements are based on historical costs, and the omission of the market value of assets is a deceiving factor. A balance sheet based on historical costs might not be an accurate *snapshot* of a company's financial position. The appreciation of assets gives company leaders leverage to increase the amount of cash reinvested in the company, and it is not recorded on the financial statements.

Restatement of Research Question and Hypotheses

The current study was conducted with a quantitative research design to examine how the hidden market value of assets affects stakeholders. Correlation analyses were used to examine relationships among variables and to test hypotheses (Zikmund, 2003). Independent -samples t-test were used to investigate the two independent groups, female participants and male participants (SPSS, 2005; Zikmund, 2003). The question of whether the hidden power in the market value of assets affects stakeholders' investment decisions was addressed.

In order to answer the research question, two hypotheses were tested:

H10: The appreciation value of assets will not be used by either female or male stakeholders to make decisions regarding borrowing cash for capital or operating expenditure.

H1A: The appreciation value of assets will be used by either female or male stakeholders to make decisions regarding borrowing cash for capital or operating expenditure.

H20: The market value of assets will not help either female or male investors make better investment decisions.

H2A: The market value of assets will help either female or male investors make better investment decisions.

Description of Research Design

Constructs. Fair market value of assets is defined as the amount that could be received on the sale of an asset (Siegel & Shim, 2005). Appreciation value is the amount of increase in the value of assets (Siegel & Shim, 2005). The purpose of the study was to determine whether stakeholders use appreciation and fair market value of assets when making investment decisions.

The accounting model. The ratios that are important for investors are those that concern the relationship between dividends and market values.

Previous literature has argued the fair value of assets should be used instead of the historical cost principle of accounting in financial statements (Benston & Wall, 2005; Poon, 2004). Managers can declare and pay dividends to common stockholders when they accumulate earnings. Investors rely on financial statements to make sound judgments regarding the value of their investments. According to Baker, Powell, and Veit (2002), managers stress the importance of maintaining dividend continuity and agree that changes in dividends affect firm value. Investors want higher regular dividends

(Baker, Mukherjee, & Powell, 2005). Accordingly, organizational leaders and investors are concerned about the bottom line (i.e., dividends).

Investors rely on the ratios that indicate market trends, liquidity, profitability, and solvency of the company to ensure their return on investments and the dividends they expect to receive are stable and reasonably secured. The users of financial statements rely on financial statement analysis to make informed decisions in pursuing their own goals (Larson et al., 2005). Furthermore, investors are likely to rely heavily on public disclosure by borrowers regarding performance and future prospects (Ma umdar & Sengupta, 2005).

The ratios that are important to investor's concern dividends and market values, and investors rely on these ratios in two ways to measure returns on the investments. The first approach is to divide the market price per-share of common stock by the amount of the earnings-per-share, a method known as the Price-Earnings Ratio or Earnings Yield (Weygandt et al., 2003). The second measurement is based on Dividend Yield. In the Dividend Yield, the investor divides the dividend per share of common stock by the current market price per share (Horngren & Harrison, 1989).

The ratios used in the context of the current study explain the importance of the market prices when making a sound judgment about investing in certain stocks. Dividend Yield is based on the view that market prices are an essential component for deciding on the purchase of stocks and describes the economic event that is involved. The calculation for both types of ratios is based on the market value, but market value is an essential component of the accounting transactions and monetary transactions (Weygandt et at., 2003).

Scholars and accounting practitioners have claimed corporations have calculated Earnings-to-Book ratio (EtB) by dividing earnings per share by the book value per share (Abacus Wealth Partners, LLC, 2003; Martikainen, 1997). In normal circumstances, the returns of EtB are much higher than the Earnings Yield. Investors are not concerned about the relationship between earnings per share and the book value per share, but investors are concerned about the relationship between the current market price per share and the earnings per share, along with the relationship between the dividend per share and the current price per share, which reflects the current market prices (larson et al., 2005).

For the purpose of the current study, it was assumed that EtB ratio has been used occasionally in accounting literature for comparison with Earnings-to-Market. The EtB ratio has been rarely utilized because it includes the book value per share, which is not important in investors' decisions. The argument in favor of using the market price as an indicator for investors might prove to be more significant than the book value.

The Earnings Yield or Price Earnings ratio is the ratio of the market price of a share of common stock to the company's earnings per share (Horngren & Harrison, 1989). The Earnings Yield or Price Earnings ratio is important because the market price is an essential factor for investors' decision making or users of financial statements in general (Horngren & Harrison, 1989). The current study was based on the assumption investors are among the users of financial statements and they should be able to make decisions regarding when to invest in a company.

The market price of a share of stock is used in both the EtB ratio and the Earnings Yield or Price Earnings ratio and is involved in the actual financial position of a company. To obtain Dividend Yield is to divide dividend-per-share by the current market price-per-share. Accordingly, the return on assets should be calculated by dividing the current fair value of net income by the average total current fair value of assets in order to reflect the correct return on the investment. The current study was based on the argument individuals who compile financial statements should use the fair value, and management should use these financial statements.

Description of Materials and Instruments

A survey was administered via the Internet. There were significant advantages to using the Internet to conduct a survey and recruit participants. The data collection instrument reached a large number of potential participants with relative ease (Bordens & Abbott, 2002). Surveys provide a quick, inexpensive, efficient, and accurate means of assessing information about a population. Since the mid-20th century, particularly since the 1980s, survey research techniques and standards have become scientific and accurate (Trochim, 2001).

Procedures

The variable of gender was included in the survey in order to determine potential differences in investing trends between genders. The questionnaire was constructed using a Likert-type scale that allowed respondents to indicate how strongly they agreed or disagreed with carefully constructed statements that ranged from very positive to very negative toward an attitudinal object. Seven items were included in the survey:

Item1: I recommend the use of assets as collateral to generate capital.

Item2: I recommend the use of the equity of a property to generate capital.

Item3: I recommend the use of traditional depreciation methods to determine replacement costs.

Item4: As an investor, I think that the market value of the company's assets helps me in my investment decisions.

Item5: As an investor, I am aware of the market value of the assets of the company in which I own stock.

Item6: As an investor, I think that I need to know the current market value of the company's assets to make better investment decisions. Item7: I think that the company should pay property taxes on the appreciated value of its assets.

Ethical Assurances

In the current research, there was no financial or physical risk to the participants by participating in the survey. Participation was anonymous, and the names of the participants were not recorded in order to maintain confidentiality. The items were easy statements for the participants to ensure understanding of the items and the data are gathered by a third party. There was a single purpose for the study: Measuring the differences between the genders in the investing decisions. No deception was used regarding the purpose of conducting the survey (Creswell, 2003). The third party who gathered the data was Vovici's EFM Feedback, an award-winning survey solution for creating, conducting, and analyzing online surveys in a secure, hosted environment. The survey was reviewed by a research consultant/statistician to correct for irregularities that might rise from using a third party.

The survey was submitted to the Northcentral University Ethics Committee before distribution to the participants to make sure the committee was well-informed. The items in the questionnaire were formulated clearly and were easy to answer. The items were multiple response. The gender variable was included as an independent variable to compare investment trends between males and females (Rodrigues & Rodrigues, 2003). Gender was used to measure the differences between the investing decisions made by the male participants and the female participants. Measuring the behavior of the female and male participants may help the individuals make better investing decisions based on the natural behavior between males and females.

Survey items were designed and tested before the final study to ensure the reliability and validity of the items. A pilot test was conducted to establish trust and respect with the participants before the final study. The pilot test was done among friends and family members of the researcher. The pilot participants' comments were incorporated in the revision of the final instrument (Creswell, 2003). An outside research consultant/ statistician was consulted to ensure the data were free of researcher bias and valid for analysis. An informed consent statement was developed, and the participants were free to complete or not to complete the survey (Creswell, 2003).

The items were short, clear, straightforward, and contained no hidden meanings; and they focused on the opinion of participants toward investing decisions. The items were presented to the participants in sequence. The structure of the questionnaire was a five-point Likert-type scale (Trochim, 2001). During the interpretation of data, accurate accounts of the participants' answers were necessary, possibly requiring debriefing with the participants. The researcher's email was provided to participants to answer any questions (Creswell, 2003).

The purpose of the research was to describe behavioral patterns in investment decisions by stakeholders. Sample selection error occurred because of the choice of Internet distribution of the survey. But to avoid the random sampling error, the sample size was increased (Zikmund, 2003); and determining the sample error and the Total Sample Size were conducted by using GPower software.

Chapter 4

FINDINGS

Overview

One research question was a guide for this research: How does the hidden market value of assets affect male and female stakeholders' investment decisions?

The research was conducted and the hypotheses were tested according to the quantitative research design to examine how the hidden market value of assets affected stakeholders. Correlational analyses were used to examine the relationships among variables and to test hypotheses. Independent -samples t-test is used to investigate differences between two independent groups, female participants and male participants. The question of whether the hidden power in the market value of assets affects stakeholders' investment decisions was addressed.

In order to answer the research question, the following hypotheses were tested:

H10: The appreciation vaiue of assets will not be used by either female or male stakeholders to make decisions regarding borrowing cash for capital or operating expenditure. According to the findings this null hypothesis was rejected.

H1A: The appreciation value of assets will be used by either female or male stakeholders to make decisions regarding borrowing cash for capital or operating expenditure. There is a trend among the participants to support this alternative hypothesis.

H2o: The market value of assets will not help either female or male investors make better investment decisions. This null hypothesis also is rejected because the participants were aware and should be aware of the fair market value of the assets.

H2A: The market value of assets will help either female or male investors make better investment decisions. The tendency among participants was that the awareness of the market value of assets is an important component when it comes to the investment decisions.

This chapter is divided to a findings section and a section on the analysis and evaluation of the findings. A survey was administered via the Internet. There were significant advantages to using the Internet to conduct a survey and recruit participants. The data collection instrument reached a large number of participants with relative ease. The survey provided a quick, inexpensive, efficient, and accurate means of assessing information about a population.

Gender was included as an independent variable in the survey in order to determine potentialdifferences in investing trends between genders. The questionnaires were constructed using a Likert-type scale that allowed respondents to indicate how strongly they agreed or disagreed with carefully constructed statements that ranged from very positive to very negative toward an attitudinal object. There were a total of 519 participants (225 female, 289 male) who responded to the survey.

Findings

The research question aimed to examine: How the hidden market value of assets affected male and female stakeholders' investment decisions. In order to address the hypotheses, the responses to the five- point Likert-type scale were converted into numerical codes (1=strongly disagree, 2=disagree, 3=neutral, 4=agree, and 5=strongly agree). As will be outlined in specific detail below, both female and male respondents agreed that the market value of assets helps them make better investment decisions. The participants equally shared the need to know the current market value of the company's assets to make better investment decisions.

Analysis and Evaluation of Findings

Table 1

Group Statistics

Item	Gender	N	M	SO
Item 1	Female	225	3.52	1.06
	Male	289	3.60	1.12
Item 2	Female	225	3.51	1.16
	Male	289	3.42	1.21
Item 3	Female	223	3.21	1.11
	Male	288	3.41	1.12
Item4	Female	222	3.76	0.96
	Male	288	3.89	0.98
Item 5	Female	226	3.54	1.21
	Male	290	3.62	1.12
Item 6	Female	223	4.06	1.07
	Male	287	4.04	1.01
Item 7	Female	222	3.29	1.17
	Male	290	3.14	1.33

Table 1and 2 show that female participants were not significantly different from male participants on Item 1 to 7. Inspection of the two group means indicates that the average Likert Scale codes (1 strongly disagree, 2 disagree, 3 neutral, 4 agree, and 5 strongly agree) for female participants for Item 1 (M = 3.52) is not significantly lower than the points (M = 3.60) for males. The difference between the means is 0.08 points on a 5 point scale. The effective sized is approximately .07. On the other hand, the result is zero, which lies between the upper and the lower limits (see Table 2) in all7 Items. The lower limit of the confidence interval on Item 1 tells us that the difference between females and males could be as small as -.276 points out of 5 (Morgan, Leech, Gloeckner, and Barrett, 2007).

Table 2

Independent Samples t-test Results

		Levene's Test for Equality of Variances		t-test for Equality of Means						95% CI of the Difference	
		F	p	T	Of	p Difference	M Difference	SE Difference		Lower	Upper
Item 1	Equal var. assumed	0.45	.50	-0.88	512.00	.38	-0.09	0.10		-0.28	0.10
	Equal var. not assumed			-0.89	493.46	.38	-0.09	0.10		-0.27	0.10
Item 2	Equal var. assumed	0.92	.34	0.84	512.00	.40	0.09	0.11		-0.12	0.30
	Equalvar. not assumed			0.84	490.88	.40	0.09	0.10		-0.12	0.30
Item 3	Equalvar. assumed	0.16	.68	-1.92	509.00	.05	-0.19	0.10		-0.39	0.004
	Equal var. not assumed			-1.92	480.68	.05	-0.19	0.10		-0.39	0.004
Item 4	Equalvar. assumed	0.001	.98	-1.52	508.00	.13	-0.13	0.09		-0.30	0.04
	Equal var. not assumed			-1.52	481.63	.13	-0.13	0.09		-0.30	0.04
Item 5	Equalvar. assumed	2.81	.09	-0.77	514.00	.44	-0.08	0.10		-0.28	0.12
	Equal var. not assumed			-0.77	464.83	.44	-0.08	0.10		-0.28	0.12
Item 6	Equalvar. assumed	0.30	.59	0.26	508.00	.79	0.02	0.09		-0.16	0.21
	Equalvar. not assumed			0.26	464.28	.79	0.02	0.09		-0.16	0.21
Item 7	Equalvar. assumed	6.97	.009	1.37	510.00	.17	0.15	0.11		-0.07	0.38
	Equalvar. not assumed			1.40	499.76	.16	0.15	0.11		-0.06	0.37

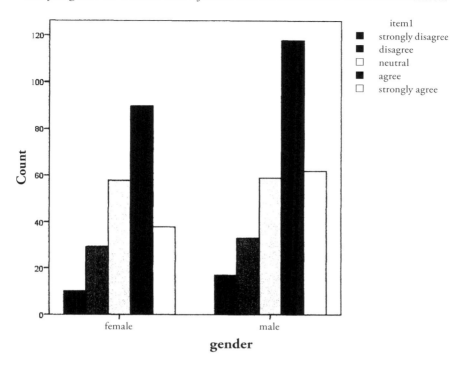

Figure 1. Item1: **I** recommend the use of assets as collateral to generate capital.

Table 3

The Percentage of Females and Males Regarding Item 1

Item 1	Female	Male
1	4.4% (10)	5.9% (17)
2	12.9% (29)	11.4% (33)
3	25.8% (58)	20.4% (59)
4	40.0% (90)	40.8% (118)
5	16.9% (38)	21.5% (62)
Total Counts	225	289

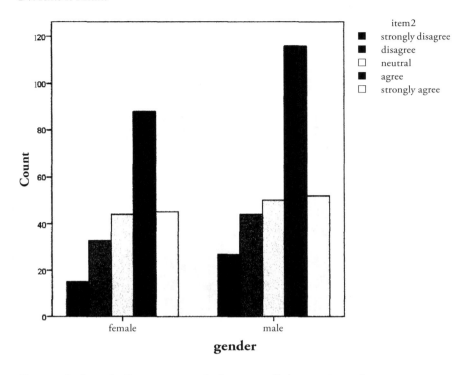

Figure 2. ltem2: I recommend the use of the equity of a property to generate capital.

Table 4

The Percentage of Females and Males Regarding Item 2

ltem2	Female	Male
1	6.7% (15)	9.3% (27)
2	14.7% (33)	15.2% (44)
3	19.6% (44)	17.3% (50)
4	39.1% (88)	40.1% (116)
5	20.0% (45)	18.0% (52)
Total Counts	225	289

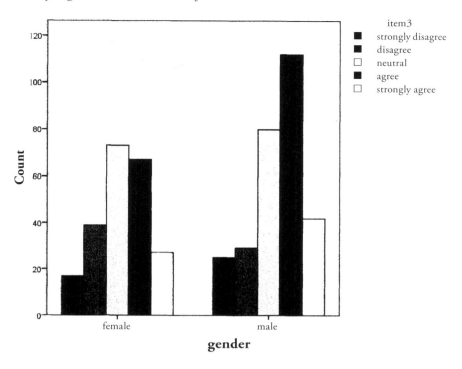

Figure 3. ltem3: **I** recommend the use of traditional depreciation methods to determine replacement costs.

Table 5

The Percentage of Females and Males Regarding Item 3

Item 3	Female	Male
1	7.6°/o {17)	8.7°/o (25)
2	17.5°/o (39)	10.1% (29)
3	32.7°/o (73)	27.8°/o (80)
4	30.0°/o (67)	38.9°/o {112)
5	12.1°/o {27)	14.6°/o {42)
Total Counts	223	288

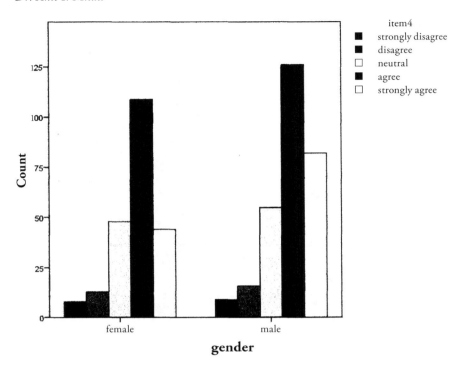

Figure 4. ltem4: As an investor, I think that the market value of the company's assets helps me in my investment decisions.

Table 6

The Percentage of Females and Males Regarding Item 4

ltem4	Female	Male
1	3.6% (8)	3.1% (9)
2	5.9% (13)	5.6% (16)
3	21.6% (48)	19.1%(55)
4	49.1% (109)	43.8% (126)
5	19.8% (44)	28.5% (82)
Total Counts	222	288

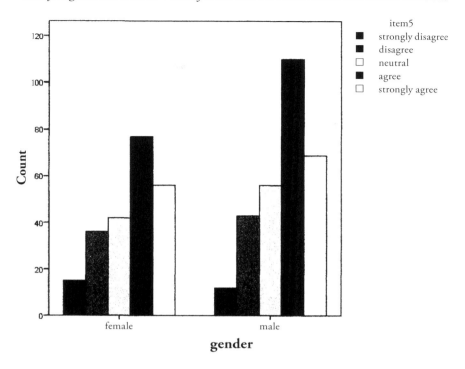

Figure 5. ltem5: As an investor, I am aware of the market value of the assets of the company in which I own stock.

Table 7

The Percentage of Females and Males Regarding Item 5

Item 5	Female	Male
1	6.6% (15)	4.1%(12)
2	15.9% (36)	14.8% (43)
3	18.6% (42)	19.3% (56)
4	34.1% (77)	37.9% (110)
5	24.8% (56)	23.8% (69)
Total Counts	226	290

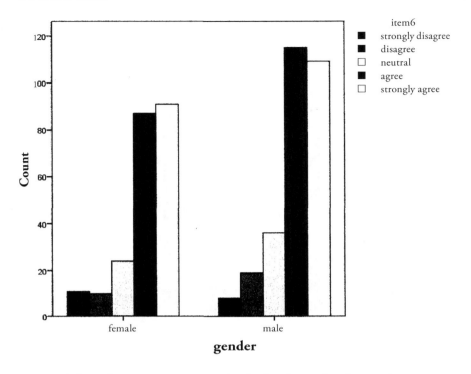

Figure 6. ltem6: As an investor, I think that I need to know the current market value of the company's assets to make better investment decisions.

Table 8

The Percentage of Females and Males Regarding Item 6

ltem6	Female	Male
1	4.9% (11)	2.8% (8)
2	4.5% (10)	S.S% (10)
3	10.8% (24)	12.5% (36)
4	39.0% (87)	40.1% (115)
5	40.8% (91)	38.0% (109)
Total Counts	223	287

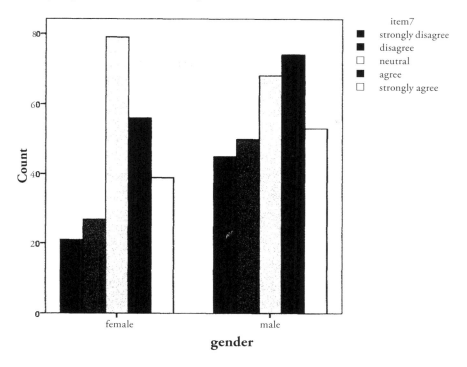

Figure 7. ltem7: **I** think that the company should pay property taxes on the appreciated value of its assets.

Table 9

The Percentage of Females and Males Regarding Item 7

ltem7	Female	Male
1	9.5% (21)	15.5% (45)
2	12.2% (27)	17.2% (50)
3	35.6% (79)	23.4% (68)
4	25.2% (56)	25.5% (74)
5	17.6% (39)	18.3% (53)
Total Counts	222	290

Summary

The appreciation of assets is the manifestation of the market forces that affect the assets' value {Chen & Wei, 1993). Investors need to know the fair value of assets of companies in order to realistically evaluate their investments. The survey positively answered the research question. Both female and male respondents agreed the market value of assets helps them make better investment decisions. The participants equally shared the need to know the current market value of the company's assets to make better investment decisions. The investment decisions were shared evenly by the female and male respondents.

Chapter 5

CONCLUSIONS AND RECOMMENDATIONS

Conclusions

This dissertation was designed to investigate the relationship between the fair market value of assets and stakeholders' investment decisions. According to the FASB, GAAP require disclosing the fair value of assets of organizations. This research investigated the effect of the disclosure of fair value of assets on stakeholders' investment decisions.

Financial statements are based on historical costs, and the omission of the market value of assets is a deceiving factor. A balance sheet based on historical costs might not be an accurate *snapshot* of a company's financial position. The appreciation of assets gives company leaders leverage to increase the amount of cash reinvested in the company, and it is not recorded on the financial statements.

The research question aimed to examine: How the hidden market value of assets affected male and female stakeholders' investment decisions. The survey positively answered this question. Both female and male respondents, total519 participants, agreed the market value of assets helps them make better investment decisions. The participants equally shared the need to know the current market value of the company's assets to make better investment decisions.

In order to answer the research question, the following hypotheses were tested:

H1a: The appreciation value of ass ts will not be used by either female or male stakeholders to make decisions regarding borrowing cash for capital or operating expenditure. According to the findings this null hypothesis was rejected.

H1A: The appreciation value of assets will be used by either female or male stakeholders to make decisions regarding borrowing cash for capital or operating expenditure. There is a trend among the participants to support this alternative hypothesis.

H2o: The market value of assets will not help either female or male investors make better investment decisions. This null hypothesis also is rejected because the participants were aware and should be aware of the fair market value of the assets.

H2A: The market value of assets will help either female or male investors make better investment decisions. The tendency among participants was that the awareness of the market value of assets is an important component when it comes to the investment decisions.

Investors look for concrete, useful information (Ernst & Young, 2005).

Reported earnings are confusing because the reality of the appreciated assets and the appreciation value allocation is ignored in the recent accounting principles issued by the GAAP. The appreciated value of an asset is useful information that should contribute to the logic underlying the investors' decisions. The purpose of the study was to determine whether stakeholders use appreciation and fair market value of assets when making investment decisions. The findings indicated both female and male respondents agreed the market value of assets helps them make better investment decisions.

Recommendations

Market capitalization is an indicator of the latest value of a company in the stock market and it is a good measure of the company's health. In many cases the market capitalization is dropped as seen in the recent months and during the recession. During a recession, the stock value reaches low prices and encourages a hostile-take-over by another company. In this case, the low prices of the stocks do not reflect the fair value of assets during the recession.

The fair value of assets should be estimated and the financial statements should be prepared by the companies according the fair value of assets to have a real financial position even though the prices of their stock in the stock market are down. The fair value financial statements should be the actual figures. which the investors need to read before making investing decisions. The respondents to the survey agreed the fair market value of assets is the decisive figures for the investing decisions.

References

Abacus Wealth Partners, LLC. (2003). *Earning to book ratio.* Retrieved from http://www.abacuswealth.com/resources/glossary.asp#E

Anonymous. (2003). SAS no. 101-auditing fair value measurements and disclosures. *Journal of Accountancy,* 195(6), 103-110. Retrieved March 30, 2007, from ProQuest database.

Baker, H., Powell, G., & Veit, T. (2002). Revisiting managerial perspectives on dividends policy. *Journal of Accounting and Finance,* 26(3), 267-284. Retrieved March 5, 2007, from ProQuest database.

Baker, H., Mukherjee, T., & Powell, G. (2005). Distributing excess cash: The role of specially designated dividends. *Financial Service Review,* 14(2), 111-131. Retrieved March 5, 2007, from ProQuest database.

Barefield, R., & Comiskey, E. (1971). Depreciation policy and the behavior corporate profrts. *Journal of Accounting Research,* 351-359. Retrieved March 5, 2007, from ProQuest database.

Barth, M., & Landsman, W. (1995}. Fundamental issues related to using fair value accounting for financial reporting. *Accounting Horizons,* 9(4), 97-108. Retrieved March 30, 2007, from ProQuest database.

Benston, G., & Wall, L. (2005). How should banks account for loan losses? *Economic Review-Federal Reserve Bank of Atlanta,* 90(4), 19-40. Retrieved March 30, 2007, from ProQuest database.

Black, R. (1997). Market value accounting: Panacea or poison for the banking industry? (Part 1).*The Journal of Bank Cost & Management Accounting,* 10(2}, 49-67. Retrieved March 30, 2007, from ProQuest database.

Bloom, G., Weimer, A., & Fisher, J. (1982). *Real estate.* New York: John Wiley & Sons.

Bordens, K., & Abbott, B. (2002). *Research design and methods.* New York: McGraw-Hill.

Botosan, C., Ashbaugh, H., Beatty, A. L., Davis-Friday, P. Y., Hopkins, P. E., Nelson, K. K., et al. (2005}. Response to the FASB's exposure draft on fair value measurements. *Accounting Horizons,* 19(3}, 187-197. Retrieved March 30, 2007, from ProQuest database.

Brigham, E., & Gapenski, L (1994). *Financial Management.* Dayden, FL: The Dayden Press.

Chawla, G. (2003). United States versus international financial statements. *Journal of American Academy of Business, Cambridge,* 2(2), 538-545. Retrieved March 30, 2007, from ProQuest database.

Chen, K., & Wei, K. (1993). Creditors' decisions to waive violations of accounting-based debt covenants. *The Accounting Review,* 68(2), 218-233. Retrieved March 5, 2007, from ProQuest database.

Cole, W. (2004). Our outdated accounting. *HaNard Business Review,* 23(4), 478-489.

Creswell, J. (2003). *Research design: Qualitative, quantitative, and mixed methods approaches* (2nd ed.). Thousand Oaks, CA: Sage Publications.

Devine, T. (2002). Depreciation and income measurement. *The Accounting Review,* 19(1), 39-47.

Downes, J., & Goodman, J. (2006). *Dictionary of finance and investment terms.* New York: Barron's Educational Series.

Elifoglu, 1., & Fitzsimons, A. (2004). FASB proposes new guidance on fair value measurements.*Commercial Lending Review,* 19(6), 37-44. Retrieved March 30, 2007, from ProQuest database.

Ernst & Young. (2005). *Effect of adopting /AS: 2002-2005.* Retrieved March 30, 2007, from http://www.ey.com/GLOBAUcontent. nsfllnternational/Assurance_-_IAS_-_Effects_of_Adopting_IAS_ 2002_-_2005

Fairfield, P., Whisenant, J., & Yohn, T. (2003). Accrued earnings and growth: Implication for future profitability and market mispricing. *The Accounting Review,* 78(1), 353-371.

Fargher, N. (2001). Management perceptions of fair-value accounting for all financial instruments. *Australian Accounting Review,* 11(2), 62-73. Retrieved March 30, 2007, from ProQuest database.

Gonedes, N. (1981). Evidence on the tax effects of inflation under historical cost accounting methods. *Journal of Business,* 54(2), 277-244. Retrieved March 5, 2007, from ProQuest database.

Haddad, A., Nathur, 1., Rangan, N., & Tadisina, S. (1993). Examining the market reactions to regulatory accounting events. *Journal of Applied Business Research,* 9(3), 36-44. Retrieved March 5, 2007, from ProQuest database.

Horngren, C., & Harrison, W. (1989). *Accounting.* Upper Saddle River, NJ: Prentice Hall.

Howe, K., & Harvey, L. (1987). Inflation and asset life: The darby versus the Fisher effect. *Journal of Financial and Quantitative Analysis,* 22(2), 249-258. Retrieved March 5, 2007, from ProQuest database.

Kempner, J. (2002). Revaluation and depreciation of plant assets. *The Accounting Review,* 27(4), 506-513.

Kieso, D., Weygandt, J., & Warfield, T. (2007). *Intermediate accounting.* New York: John Wiley & Sons.

King, A. (2003). Fair value accounting: Its time has come and gone. *Strategic Finance,* 85(3), 54-57. Retrieved March 5, 2007, from ProQuest database.

Larson, K., Wild, J., & Chiappetta, B. (2005). *Fundamental accounting principles* (17th eel.). New York: McGraw-Hill.

lee, B., Press, E., & Choi, B. (2001). Capital assets and financial statement distortion. *Competitiveness Review, 11(2),* 57-74. Retrieved March 5, 2007, from ProQuest database.

lev, B. (1990). On the usefulness of earnings and earning research: Lessons and directions from two decades of empirical research [Supplement]. *Journal of Accounting Research, 2,* 153-201.

MacDonald, L., & Richardson, A. (2002). Alternative perspectives on the development of American management accounting: Relevance lost induces a renaissance. *Journal of Accounting Literature, 2,* 120-157. Retrieved March 5, 2007, from ProQuest database.

Martikainen, M. (1997). Accounting losses and investors' growth expectations. *International Review of Financial Analysis,* 6(2), 97-106. Retrieved March 5, 2007, from ProQuest database.

Mason, P. (2002). Accounting for current depreciation. *The Accounting Review,* 5(2), 106-110.

Mazumdar, S., & Sengupta, P. (2005). Disclosure and the loan spread on private debt. *Financial Analysts Journal,* 61(3), 83-96. Retrieved March 5, 2007, from ProQuest database.

McNichols, T. (1954). Adjustment of fixed assets to reflect price level changes. *Accounting Review,* 29(1), 106-114.

Miller, M., & Loftus, J. (2000). Measurement entering the 21ˢᵗ century: A clear or blocked road ahead? *Australian Accounting Review,* 10(2), 4-19. Retrieved March 30, 2007, from ProQuest database.

Morgan, G., Leech, N., Gloeckner, G., & Barrett (2007). Spss *for introductory Statistics: Use and interpretation.* New Jersey: Lawrence Erlbaum Association, Inc., Publishers

Mosich, A., & Larsen, E. (1982). *Intermediate accounting.* New York: McGraw Hill Book Company.

Nielsen, 0. (2002). Depreciation as a function of revenue. *The Accounting Review,* 13(3), 265-275.

Poon, W. (2004). Using fair value accounting for financial instruments. *American Business Review,* 21(1), 39-41. Retrieved March 30, 2007, from ProQuest database.

Ro, B. (1981). The disclosure of replacement cost accounting data and its effect on transaction volumes. *The Accounting Review,* 56(2), 70-84. Retrieved March 5, 2007, from ProQuest database.

Rodrigues, D., & Rodrigues, R. (2003) The research paper: A guide to library and internet research. Upper Saddle River: NJ: Prentice Hall..

Siegel, J., & Shim, J. (2005). *Dictionary of accounting terms.* New York: Barron's Educational Series.

SPSS15/. (2005). *Spss 15 Brief Guide.* Chicago, IL: SPSS. Trochim, W. (2001). *The research methods knowledge base.* Ohio: Thomson.

Turner, L. E. (2000). *Office of the chief accountant: Letter requesting the A/CPA to provide industry guidance on models and methodologies for valuation.* Retrieved April 11, 2007, from http://www.sec.gov/info/accountants/staffletterslvaluguid.htm

Vickman, T. (1986). Inflation's impact on financial management. *Journal of Small Business Management,* 19(1), 1-6. Retrieved April111, 2007, from ProQuest database.

Weygandt, J., Kieso, D., & Kimmel, P. (2003). *Financial accounting* (UOPHX Special Edition Series). New York: John Wiley & Sons.

Zikmund, W. (2003). *Business Research methods.* Mason, OH: Thomson.

Appendix

THE CONSENT FORM AND THE SURVEY

The Fair Value of Assets and the Investing Decisions Purpose. You are not invited to participate in this research study, The research was already conducted during year 2008. The purpose of this study is to examine the link (if any) between the fair value of assets and a person's investing decisions. It focuses on how individual investors make their decisions. There is no deception in this study. We are interested in your opinions and reflections about your life as an investor.

Participation requirements. You will be asked to complete one web page questionnaires about how you view the faire value of assets. The session will last less than 15 minutes. Research Personnel.The following people re involved in this research project and may be contacted at any time: Anis I. Milad- 410-282-8708 or aimilad@comcast.net

Potential Risk *I* Discomfort. Although there are no known risks in this study,some of the information is personally sensitive and also indudes questions about investing which may be distressing to some people. However,you may withdraw at any time and you may choose not to answer any question that you feel uncomfortable in answering.

Potential Benefit. There are no direct benefits to you of participating in this research. No incentives are offered. The results will have scientific interest that may eventually have benefits for investors.

Anonymity *1* Confidentiality. The data collected in this study are confidential. All data are coded such that your name is not associated with them.In addition,the coded data are made available only to the researchers associated with this project.

Right to Withdraw. You have the right to withdraw from the study at any time without penalty. You may omit questions on any questionnaires if you do not want to answer them. We would be happy to answer any question that my arise about the study. Please direct your questions or comments to: Anis I.Milad..•...••.....

INSTRUCTIONS

Please read each statement, then click on the number below the statement best matching your opinion about the statement.

- 1 means that you strongly disagree with the statement
- 2 means you disagree somewhat
- 3 means a neutral value of the statement
- 4 means that you agree somewhat
- 5 means that you strongly agree

1) I recommend the use of assets as collateral to generate capital.

- O 1
- O 2
- O 3
- O 4
- O 5

2) I recommend the use of the equity of a property to generate capital.

- O 1
- O 2
- O 3
- O 4
- O 5

3) I recommend the use of traditional depreciation methods to detennine replacement costs.

- O 1
- O 2
- O 3
- O 4
- O 5

4) As an investor, I think that the market value of the company's assets helps me in my investment decisions.

O 1
O 2
O 3
O 4
O 5

5) As an investor, I am aware of the market value of the assets of the company in which I own stock.

O 1
O 2
O 3
O 4
O 5

6) As an investor, I think that I need to know the mnent market value of the company's assets to make better investment decisions.

O 1
O 2
O 3
O 4
O 5

7) I think that the company should pay property taxes on the appreciated value of its assets.

O 1
O 2
O 3
O 4
O 5

8) What is your gender?
   Female = 0 Male = 1

   - ○ 0
   - ○ 1

   Thank you for your partidpation.My best wishes!!

Printed in the United States
By Bookmasters